Ole & Lena
Men Are from Uranus

Featuring

Ann Berg as Lena
with Bruce Danielson as Ole

Adventure Publications, Inc.
Cambridge, MN

PHOTO CREDITS

Cover photos by Jonathan Norberg

All other photos are copyright Ryan Jacobson

DEDICATIONS

Ann Berg: To Larry, who is a genius in the art of being a husband.

ACKNOWLEDGEMENTS

Thanks to the following people who appeared in this half of the book: Page 6: Larry Ostrom and Mike Sorn; Page 10: Dr. Lowell Becker; Page 12: Mitchell Nelson; Page 18: Larry Ostrom; Page 20: Jack Hammargren; Page 22: Larry Ostrom; Page 26: Brent Schoenwald; Page 30: Daniel Husom; Page 36: Kimberly Hale; Page 40: Katie Barnes; Page 46: Robert Bergstrom; Page 48: Brenda Cummings; Page 50: Addison Sullivan. Thanks to the following businesses and friends who lent supplies or locations and made this book possible: Cambridge-Isanti High School, Cambridge Medical Center, Guetschoff Theatre, Dana Kuznar, Larry Ostrom, Perkins Restaurant of Cambridge and Purple Hawk Golf Course. A special thank you to Ryan Jacobson for his creative, photographic and technical skills that added so much to the aesthetic quality of the photographs and the imaginative quality of the book. Your input was invaluable.

ABOUT ANN BERG

Lena has the pleasure of interviewing Ann about her new book. Here's what Ann had to say:

Lena: I'm interviewing Ann Berg, who wrote dis here book on da *Men Are from Uranus* side. Mrs. Berg, have you made some of da same mistakes I have?

Ann: I think so, Lena. After all, I got married, too.

Lena: How did you do da research on dis topic?

Ann: I have three boys, so I've been living with four boys most of my life—if you include my husband of 35 years, of course.

Lena: I take it, den, dat your boys are grown up now?

Ann: Only chronologically! And really, that's why we love them. Men bring laughter and fun into our lives.

Lena: Do you have a day job, Mrs. Berg?

Ann: I teach middle school science and reading, where a sense of humor is needed, as well.

Lena: Vat do you do in your free time, den?

Ann: I head "up north" to the cabin with my family, where I enjoy reading, gardening and playing with my "fur kid" Bailey, a bearded collie.

dey are really dumm!

Ole owns a Norwegian compass.
It shows him who's lost.

Lena: Only Ole vould tink to take toilet paper to a game of craps.

ONLY OLE (AND MEN IN GENERAL)

Ole's idea of a seven-course meal is a pizza and a six-pack of beer.

Tina: If von man can wash von stack of dishes in von hour, how many stacks of dishes can four men wash in four hours?

Lena: None. Dey'll sit down, drink beer and vatch football on television.

Lena: It's no use for a woman to tell a man to get lost. Most of dem already are.

Ole visited the newly reconstructed hospital, and he was very disappointed by what he saw.

Ole: See? I told dem if dey added a wing on da hospital, it still vouldn't be able to fly.

Lena is always relieved when Ole burps in public. After all, it could have come out the other end.

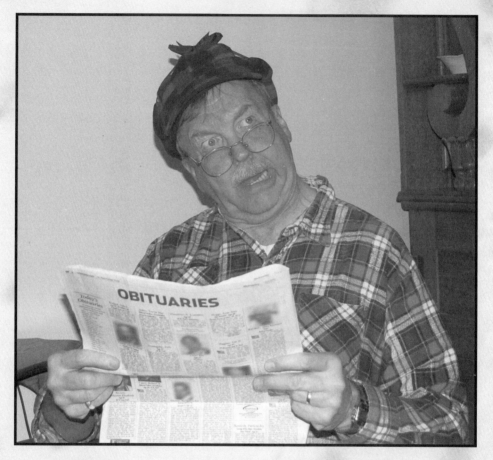

Ole: I just read da obituaries. How come everyvon dies in alphabetical order?

CLUELESS CRIMES

Ole was watching a young punk siphon gas out of a parked car. Ole turned to Lena and said, "I hope I never get dat tirsty!"

Ole fought with a mugger over 57 cents. Finally, the mugger asked why he was putting up such a fight for a measly 57 cents.

Ole replied, "So you don't find da $500 I got hidden in my shoe."

Ole and Sven both took a test, but Ole was accused of cheating. Ole became very upset that his honesty was questioned.

Ole: Just because ve both got nine right out of ten doesn't mean I copied him.

Tester: True, but on question number ten, Sven put, "I don't know," and you wrote, "Me needer."

The police accidentally arrested Ole. When they asked him to identify himself, he looked into the mirror and said, "Yah, sure, dat's me all right."

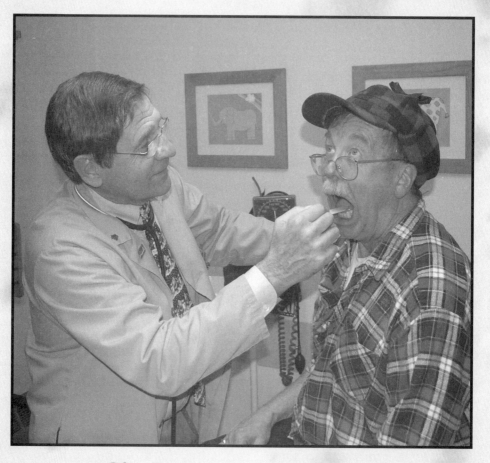

Ole: Doctor, vat's wrong vit me?

Doctor: You're sick.

Ole: I vant a second opinion.

Doctor: All right, you're stupid, as well.

MEDICAL ATTENTION

Lena ran into the dentist's office and demanded to see the dentist.

Lena: Da tooth has to be pulled. It's infected. You need to pull it now, and dere's no need for Novocain.

Dentist: Well, you're a brave woman. Which tooth is it?

Lena: Ole, come in here and show da dentist your tooth!

Ole had surgery, so the doctor told him that for a while he shouldn't use the stairway at home. At the end of the month, the doctor said it was finally okay for him to use stairs again.

Ole replied, "Tank goodness! I'm so tired of shinnying up da drain pipe to get to da bedroom."

Here are some things Ole does NOT want to hear during his surgery:

> *"Darn! Page 84 of this manual is missing!"*
>
> *"Whoa, wait a minute! If this is his spleen, then what's that?"*
>
> *"Hand me that . . . uh . . . that uh . . . thingie."*
>
> *"Better save that. We'll need it for the autopsy."*

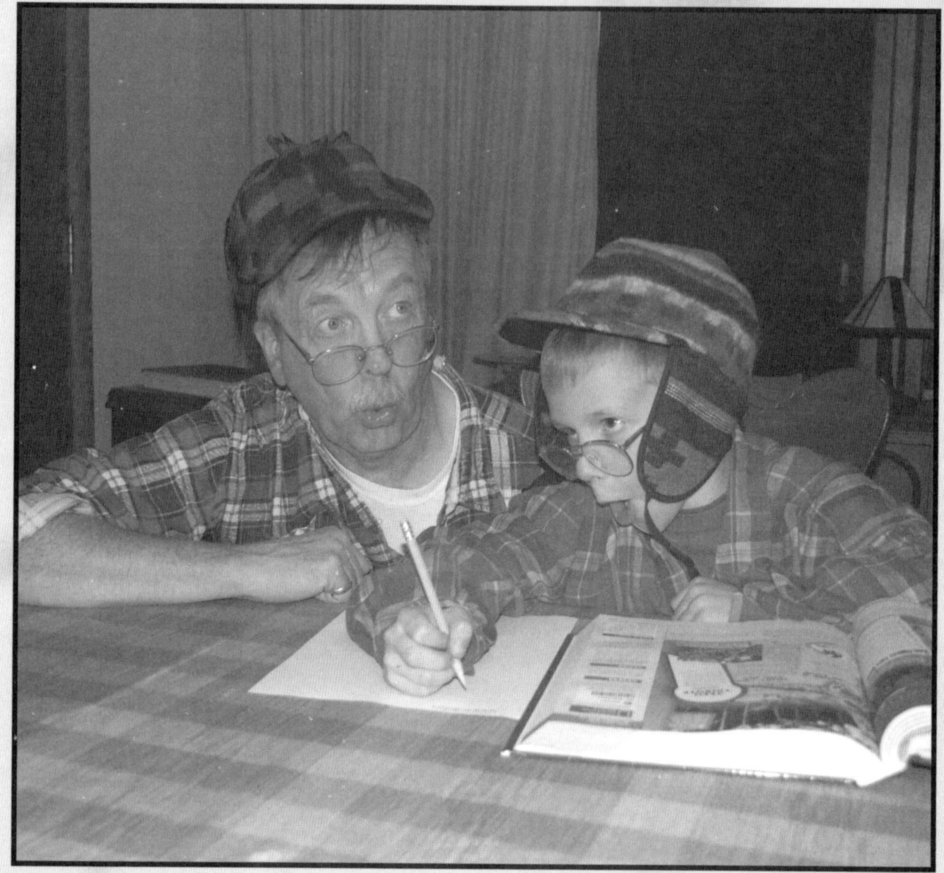

Little Ole: I found out in school today dat in some parts of Africa, a man doesn't know his vife until dey're married.

Ole: Vy single out Africa?

OLE JUNIOR

Ole Junior: Papa, da kids in turd grade make fun of me. Is it because I have such big feet or because I'm Norwegian?

Ole: Ole Junior, I tink it's because you're 19 years old.

Ole Junior: Your advice vas terrible, Papa. My girlfriend just slapped my face!

Ole: Did you tell her vat I told you? Did you tell her, "Time stands still ven I'm avay from you"?

Ole Junior: Vell, I said someting like dat. I told her dat her face vould stop a clock.

Lena: I'm glad you brushed your teeth, Ole Junior. Did you use toothpaste this time?

Ole Junior: Of course not. None of my teeth are loose!

LENA'S BUMPER STICKERS

You seem to be a few fries short of a Happy Meal.

Money isn't everything, but it sure keeps the children in touch.

Don't worry what people think. They don't do it very often.

Women who seek to be equal to men lack ambition.

I love to give homemade gifts. Which one of my kids would you like?

Everyone is entitled to my opinion.

I took an IQ test and the results were negative.

Your kid's an honor student, but you're a moron.

Lord, if I can't be skinny, please let my friends be fat.

I've been dieting for a month, but all I've lost is 31 days.

dey can relate to each
other—but not to women!

Lena: All men are idiots, and I married dere king.

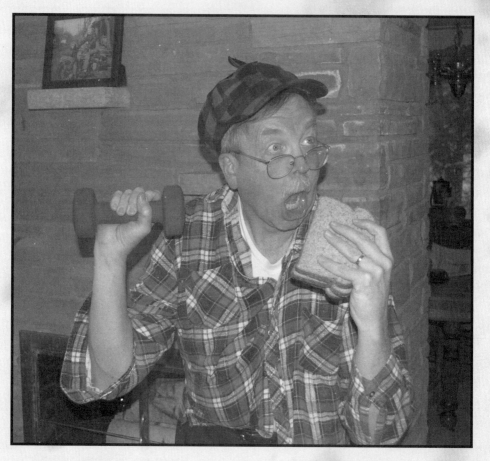

Lena: Ole had to fight hard to get da body he has. Too bad he lost.

LENA'S LAMENTS

Ole was posing before a mirror. "Lena," he said, "don't you tink my body is just dynamite?"

"Sure," answered Lena. "Too bad it's got such a short fuse."

Lena and Ole have a lot in common. For example, they were both married on the same day.

Ole bragged that no one ever boos when he speaks.

Lena replied, "Of course not. People can't boo ven dere yawning."

Lena could make her home 90% fat free if she would just throw out Ole.

When Ole Junior was born, Ole swore he was going to help with the parenting duties. So Lena asked Ole to change their son. Ole came back two hours later with a little girl.

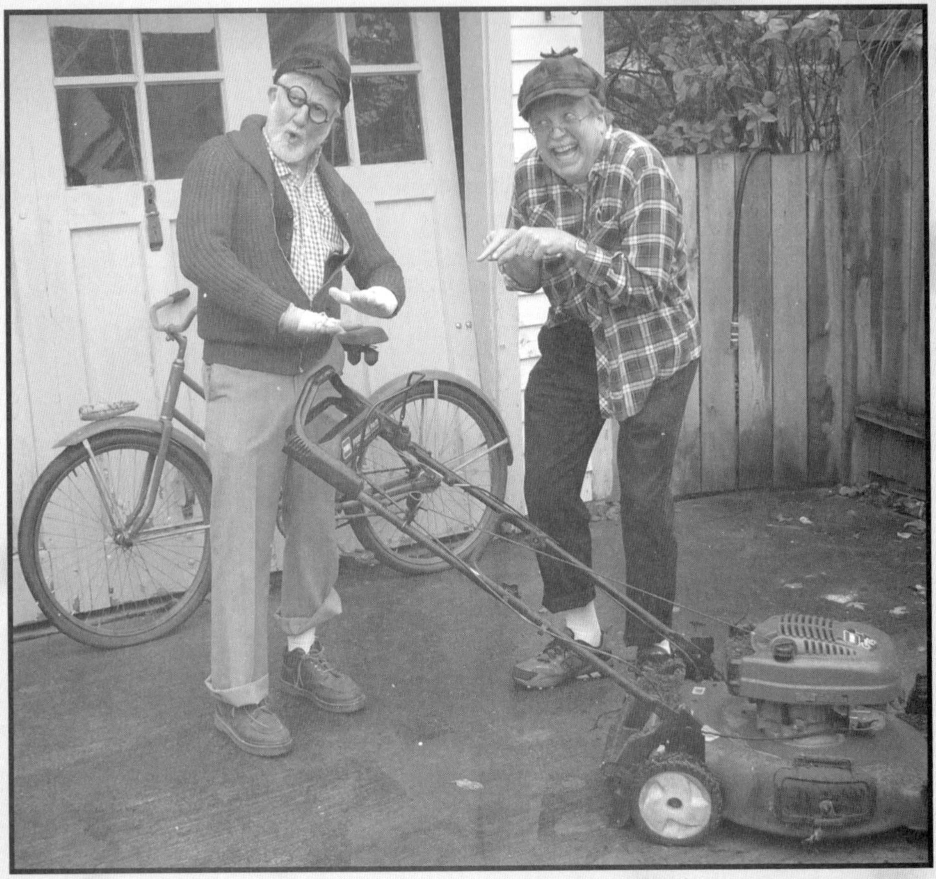

Ole: Lars, can I use your lawn mower dis afternoon?

Lars: Nah, I'm going to mow my own yard today.

Ole: Vell, okay, den could I borrow your golf clubs?

OLE'S FRIENDS

Sven: Ole, last night I dreamed I vas at Disneyland. I had da best time.

Ole: Vas I dere vit you?

Sven: No, I vas vit other friends.

Ole: Vell, last night I dreamed dat I vas out on a date vit two of da most beautiful women ever. I had dem all to myself.

Sven: Vy didn't you call me?

Ole: I did, but you vere at Disneyland.

Torvald: Ole, I left Tina for good.

Ole: I'm sorry, Torvald. Did Tina take it pretty hard?

Torvald: Oh, yah, I never knew she could sing, whistle and do cartwheels all at da same time.

Ole has some unlucky friends. Einar called the incontinence hotline, and they asked if he could hold.

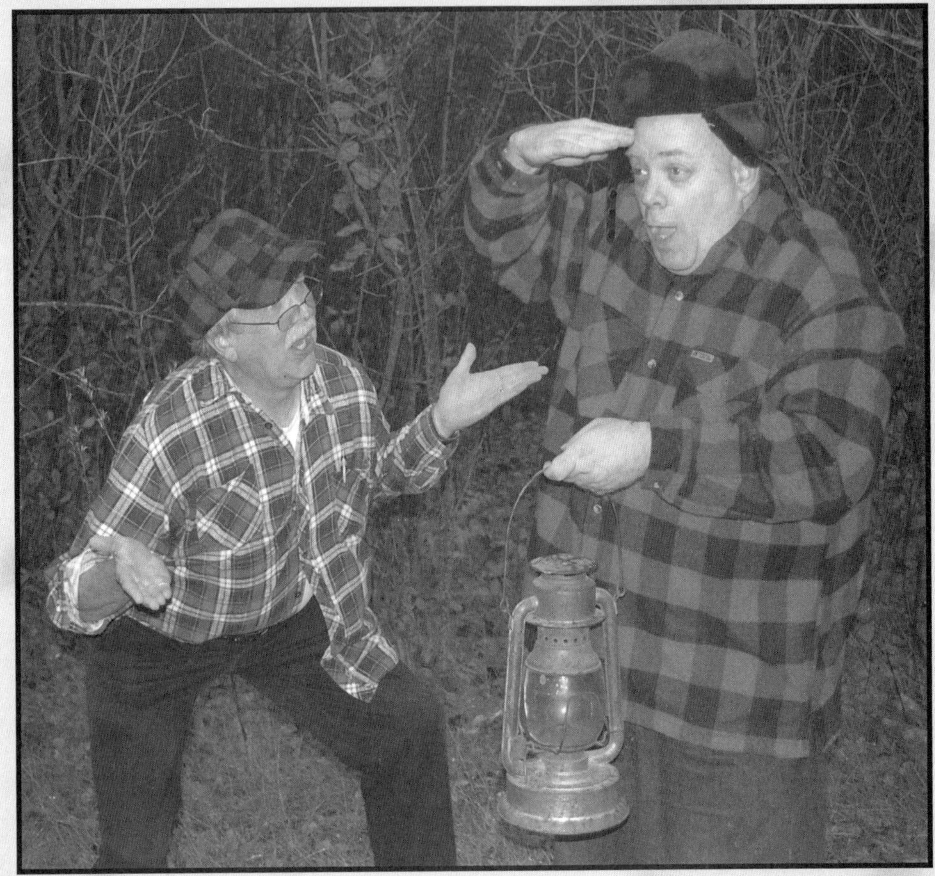

Ole: Sven, you say you're carrying a lantern to find a vife? I never carried a lantern ven I vas looking for a vife.

Sven: Yah, and look vat you got.

MARRIED LIFE

Lena: Marriage is nature's vay of keeping people from fighting vit strangers.

Ole: Torvald, on your anniversary you should tell Tina dose three little words every woman longs to hear.

Torvald: You mean, "I'll fix it"?

Lena: Dey named a shoe after Ole: the loafer.

Lena: Ole only has two faults: everyting he says and everyting he does.

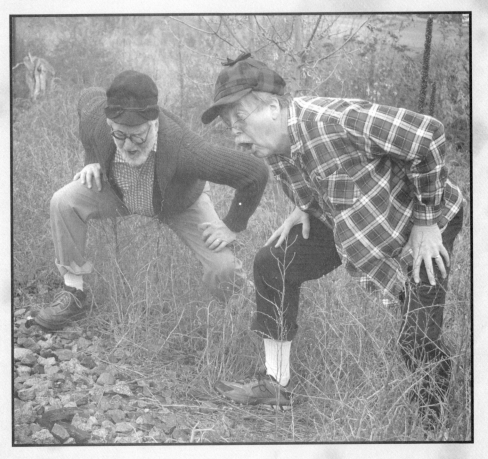

Lena: Ole and Lars vere arguing whether da tracks dey found vere bear tracks or deer tracks ven dey nearly got hit by a train.

OLE'S FAMILY

Ole's brother takes everything too literally. He read a sign that said, "Drink Canada Dry," and he headed north to try it.

One time in a restaurant, Ole's brother was choking on a nickel he had swallowed. A man rushed over and gave Olaf the Heimlich maneuver.

Ole's father was very grateful and asked the man if he was a doctor.

"Oh, no," the man said, "I'm with the IRS."

Ole: My uncle vas a psychic. He swore dat he knew da exact day and time he vas going to die.

Lena: Ole, I tink da warden told him.

When Ole's brother Olaf goes to the zoo, he needs two tickets: one to get in and one to get out.

OLE'S LATEST JOB

Ole got a job making signs for local businesses. Here were some of his ideas:

On a plumber's truck: Don't sleep vit a drip; call your plumber.

At a towing company: Ve don't charge an arm and a leg. Ve vant tows.

On a maternity room door: **Push! Push! Push!**

Outside a muffler shop: **No appointment needed; ve hear you coming.**

In a veterinarian's office: Back in five minutes. Sit! Stay!

On a proctologist's door: **To speed tings up, please back in.**

Is it any wonder the job didn't last long?

dey tink dey are romantic.
Boy, are dey foolin' demselves!

Lena asked Ole to take her somewhere expensive. He brought her to a gas station.

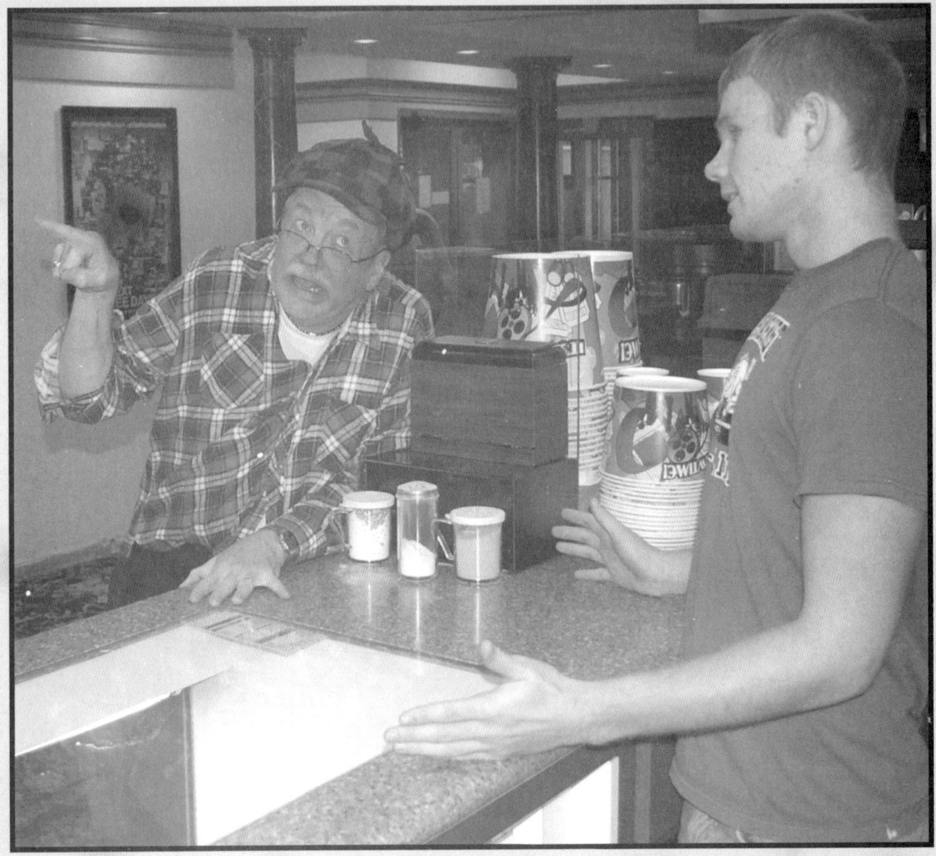

Ole: So far, I've bought six tickets to dis movie for my vife and me.

Ticketeer: Why?

Ole: Because every time I buy two tickets, dat guy over dere rips dem in half.

DATING

Ole and Lena were on a date at a restaurant, and Ole let out a loud burp after dinner. A big, burly guy walked over to the table and said, "How dare you burp like that before my wife?"

Ole sheepishly replied, "Sorry, I didn't know it vas her turn."

Lena: Ole, ven ve vere first dating, you called me all kinds of sweet names. You called me "Sweetie," "Honey" and "Cutie." How come you don't call me dose anymore?

Ole: To be honest, Lena, ven ve vere first dating, I couldn't remember your real name.

Back when Ole was single, he was very proud of his pickup lines. Here's what he'd say to a girl:

Ole: Did you fart? 'Cause you really blew me avay.

Ole: Do you have a library card? 'Cause I'd like to check you out.

Ole: If you vere a booger, I'd pick you first.

Ole: I'm Ole. Now you only have two vishes left.

On Valentine's Day, Lena's lonely aunt advertised that she wanted a man. She got a thousand responses saying, "You can have mine!"

ROMANCE

Ole: Lena says I'm not romantic, but ve go out to dinner tvice a veek. She goes on Tuesdays, and I go on Tursdays.

Lena claims that the romance is gone in their marriage. The waterbed has turned into the Dead Sea.

It looks like Ole Junior is taking after his father. He was on a date when the girl said, "Ole Junior, do you want to get in the back seat?"

"No," said Ole Junior, "I'd like to stay up here vit you."

Ole: I never made love with my vife until ve vere married. How about you?

Torvald: I don't know. Vat vas your vife's maiden name?

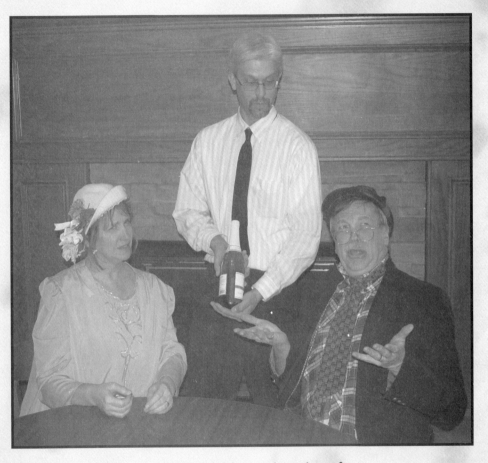

Ole: Ve vould like a bottle of vine.

Waiter: What year?

Ole: Dis year! Ve vant it vit our meal.

SEX

Lena: Ole doesn't believe in sex over 55. He says it's best to pull over to da side of da road.

Lena made Ole go to a psychiatrist. The doctor showed him ink-blot pictures and asked Ole what they made him think of. After every picture, Ole said, "Sex."

Finally, the doctor told Ole that he was very preoccupied with sex.

Ole disagreed. "You're da von showing me all dose dirty pictures."

Ole is always looking for a bargain, so he got his vasectomy at Sears. It worked great, except when Lena kisses him, the garage door goes up.

Lena: Marriage is like a midnight phone call. First you get a ring, and den you wake up.

Tina: Vat's da best vay to keep a man happy in bed?

Lena: Bring a TV into da bedroom.

LENA'S CALL-IN SHOW

Caller: How long can a man live without a brain?

Lena: Vell, Ole's over 50 now.

Caller: Lena, why don't men show their feelings?

Lena: Vat feelings?

Caller: Lena, why do men act like idiots?

Lena: Who says dey're acting?

Caller: Lena, why do men have an inferiority complex?

Lena: Vell, because dey are.

Caller: Lena, can't you ever say something kind about men?

Lena: Vell, dey are biodegradable.

OLD NORWEGIAN FRIENDS

Gustav is 92 and Carrie is 89. They are getting married soon and took a walk, stopping into the local drugstore.

Gustav: Ve're about to get married. Do you sell heart medication?

Druggist: Of course we do.

Gustav: How about suppositories?

Druggist: You bet.

Gustav: Medicine for circulation, rheumatism, arthritis and Alzheimer's?

Druggist: Yes, a large variety. The works.

Gustav: Vat about vitamins, sleeping pills and Geritol?

Druggist: Absolutely.

Gustav: Everyting for heartburn and indigestion?

Druggist: We do indeed.

Gustav: You sell veelchairs, valkers and canes?

Druggist: All speeds and sizes.

Gustav: Adult diapers?

Druggist: Sure.

Gustav: Good! Ve'd like to use dis store as our bridal registry.

dey tink dey are so charming.
Dey are losers!

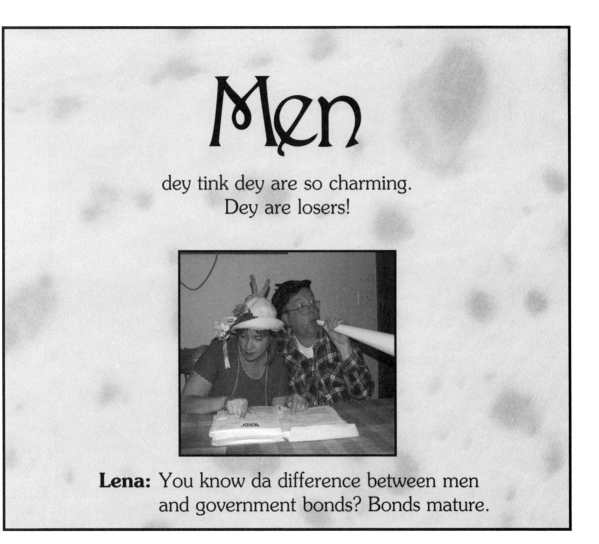

Lena: You know da difference between men and government bonds? Bonds mature.

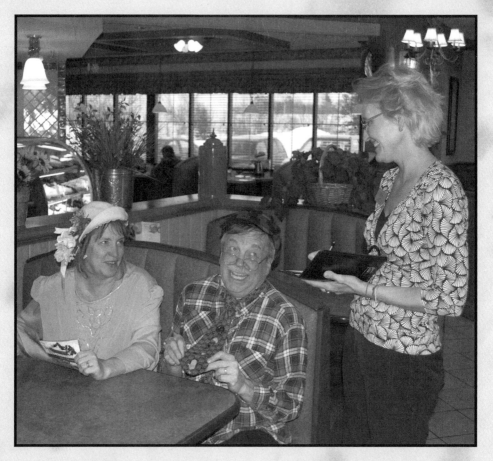

Lena: Ole keeps a record of everyting he eats. It's called his tie.

OUT & ABOUT

Lena and her friend Olga were eating at a church supper, listening to the speaker. Olga kept ogling the speaker, saying, "He looks just like my fourth husband."

"My goodness," said Lena, "how many husbands have you had?"

Olga replied, "Three."

As Ole checked into the hotel, the clerk told him the bill would be $50.

Ole: Do you take children?

Clerk: No, just cash or credit cards.

Ole's father is a well-known speaker. He can talk for hours without a note and, for that matter, without a point.

Lena: Life is a highway. Men are da speed bumps.

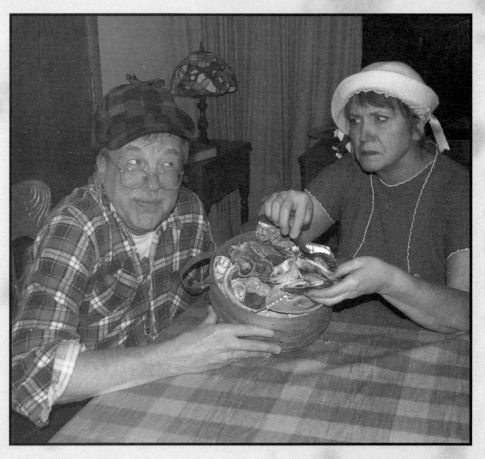

Lena asked for a pearl necklace for her birthday. Ole gave her a bushel of oysters and wished her luck.

GOOD OL' OLE

Lena: Uffda! Ole's obituary is going to be expensive. It says dey charge $1 per inch—and Ole's almost six feet tall!

Lena: Ven Ole dies, I'm burying him twelve feet under, 'cause down deep, he's a good man.

Ole has a nautical tattoo on his stomach. It used to be on his chest, but it dropped anchor.

Ole has avoided making the wrong career move; he never gets a job.

Lena: Husbands don't air dirty linen in public; dey drop it on da floor.

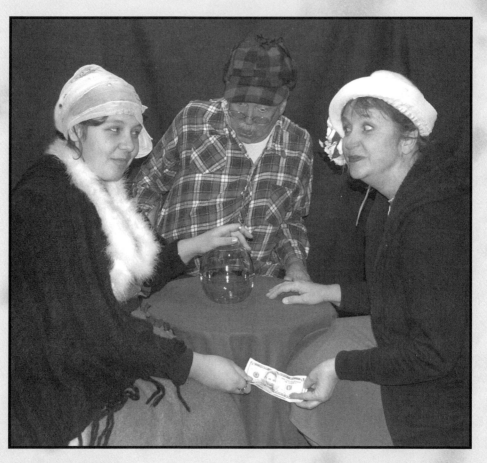

Psychic: I see you are a man who does not do a lot of cleaning. If you do not start, your future is very, very uncertain.

FAMILY MATTERS

Lena: Da babies always looked like dere father, until I turned dem right side up.

Little Lena says she thinks of herself as Snow White waiting for the Handsome Prince. But the guys she's met in school are more like Dopey, Grumpy and Sleepy.

Ole's brother Olaf has a mechanical mind. Too bad some of the screws are loose.

Ole: Women say my brother Olaf has animal magnetism.

Lena: No, Ole, dey say your brother attracts fleas.

Just before Ole's birthday, Tina asked Lena what she was getting for Ole. Lena said, "Make me an offer."

Tina: What's Ole's favorite meal?

Lena: Anyting his mother used to make.

LENA'S CALL-IN SHOW (PART 2)

Caller: Lena, my boss keeps telling me he needs some old-fashioned loving. What should I do?

Lena: Introduce him to your grandmother.

Caller: What does it mean to come home to a man who'll give you some love and tenderness?

Lena: It means you're in da wrong house.

Caller: Lena, what's the best way to get a man to go to sleep without having sex?

Lena: Dat's easy. Just say you vant to talk to him about someting very important.

Caller: How do you find out what life is like without a man around?

Lena: Get married.

JEOPARDY GAME FOR WOMEN

Category:

MEN	**ANSWER**	**QUESTION**
$10	A few good men	What are women and the Marine Corps having trouble finding?
$20	On the bedroom floor	Where can you find the best selection of men's clothing?
$30	The parting of the Red Sea, water turning to wine and a man vacuuming	What are three miracles?
$40	Three men and a baby	What happens when Ole, Sven, Lars and Torvald go fishing, and Ole catches nothing?
$50	A mental hospital	Where do you go to find a committed man?

dey are about as useful
as a screen door on a submarine!

Men are like dogs about housework. They run and hide every time they see the vacuum cleaner.

Golfer: I said, "Give me a WEDGE!"

CAREER AMBITIONS

Ole worked for a short time at a grocery store. A man came in one day and asked for half a cantaloupe. Ole told him that they only sold whole cantaloupes. The man insisted he could only use half of one and wanted Ole to check with the manager.

Ole did so but was unaware that the man followed him back to the office. Ole announced to the manager, "Ve have an idiot in da store dat vants to buy a half of da cantaloupe!" Then he noticed the man behind him, and he quickly added, "Tank goodness dis nice man is villing to buy da other half."

Ole stopped in to see his boss. "Hey, boss, ve're doing some heavy-duty housecleaning tomorrow, and Lena vants me to help out. Can I have da day off?"

"Nope," said the boss. "We're short-handed."

"Tanks," said Ole, "I knew I could count on you!"

Ole once tried his hand at acting; he played Hamlet in a community play. When the audience booed his performance, he stopped and yelled, "Don't blame me. I didn't write dis crap!"

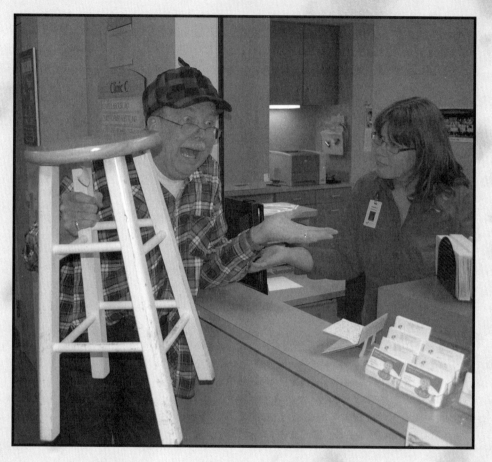

Ole is always prepared in case his doctor wants a stool sample.

DOCTOR VISITS

Doctor: Ole, I told you to take two pills and wash them down with whiskey. How's that going?

Ole: Vell, Doc, I'm two veeks behind in da pills, but I'm a month ahead vit da whiskey.

Ole: Doc, I've been limping ever since my leg surgery. Vat vould you do if you vere me?

Doctor: I'd limp too.

Doctor: Take a glass of milk before retiring.

Ole: Vat? Heck, I'm not retiring for tirty years!

Doctor: Ole, at your age, you could go at any time.

Ole: Good, Doc, 'cause I haven't gone in days.

Ole: I can't remember tings from von minute to da next.

Doctor: How long has this been going on?

Ole: How long has vat been going on?

Lena: Ole's idea of helping vit da baby vas telling me ven da diapers needed changing.

OLE'S EARLY YEARS

When Ole was little, he was so unpopular that his imaginary friend wouldn't even play with him.

Ole's hometown was so poor that their local zoo closed when the butterfly died.

Ole's house was so small that when you rang the doorbell, the toilet flushed.

Ole's family was so poor that the only way they could afford an X-ray was to lie on the luggage machine at the airport.

Ole's family was so poor that they would've had no decorations at all on their Christmas tree if Grandpa hadn't sneezed.

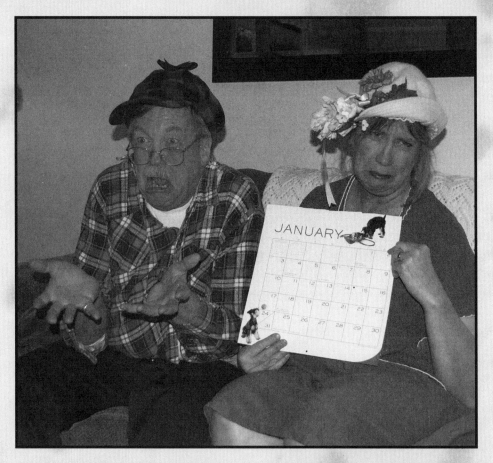

Lena: You know you're getting old ven da bank sends you a calendar von month at a time.

HUSBAND WOES

Lena was talking to her sister Ingeborg about how she met her husband.

Ingeborg: I met him at a dance, and he vas da best-looking man on da floor. I can see him now, lying dere.

Lena: After a man says, "I do," dat's da last time you'll see him do much of anyting!

Lena: It vasn't enough dat God had to make men so annoying 16 hours a day. He had to make it a clean sweep by adding snoring!

Ole and Lena were in an art museum when Ole accidentally knocked over a vase—it shattered on the floor.

An attendant rushed over. "Look what you've done. That vase was over two thousand years old!"

"Dat's okay, den," said Ole. "At least it vasn't a new von."

A fortune teller told Lena that she'd be a widow soon because her husband would die by poisoning.

Lena asked, "Vill I be acquitted?"

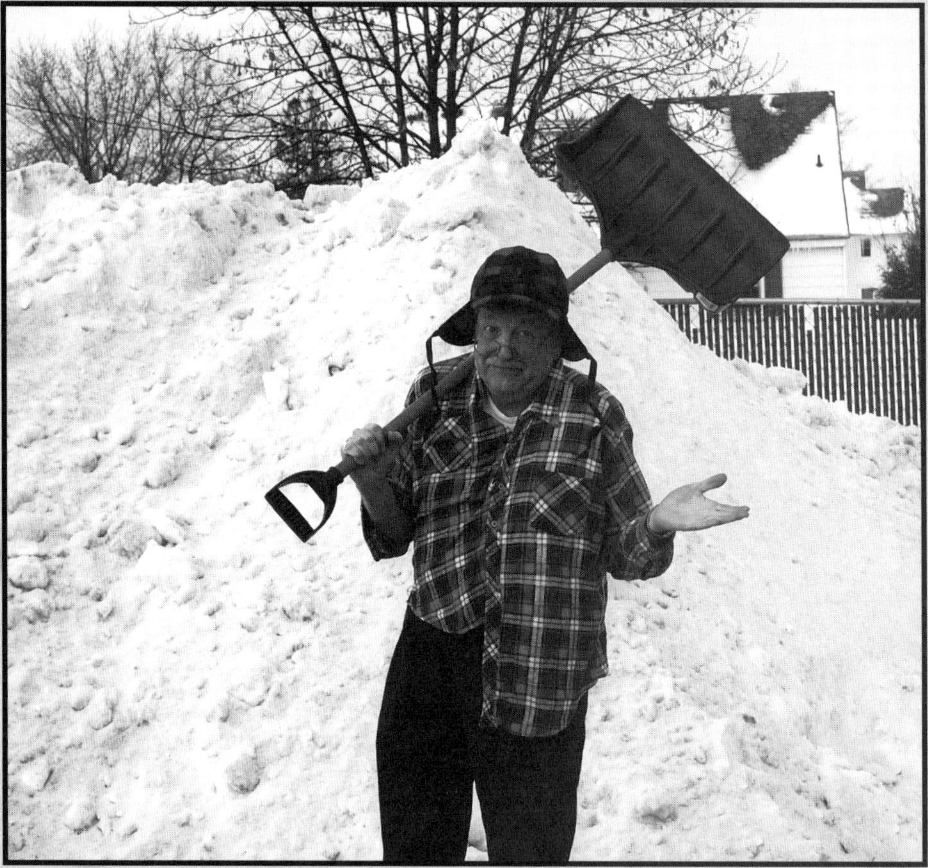

Ole: I just got word from da county. Our farm has been rezoned, and it's in Wisconsin now. Tank goodness! I swore I'd never spend another vinter in Minnesota!

HOUSEHOLD TROUBLES

Lena: Ole brags dat he's da boss in his home, but he lies about other tings, too.

Doctor: Ole, I have some bad news. You'll never be able to work again.

Ole: So vat's da bad news?

Tina: How is your pain in da neck?

Lena: He's out milking da cows.

Ingeborg: Vere is Ole?

Lena: He's at home recovering from a freak accident. He vas suddenly struck by a thought.

Ole's neighbor, Mrs. Henderson, recently lost her husband. He drowned in a vat of beer.

Ole: I'm sorry for your terrible loss, Mrs. H. I hope he vent quickly and painlessly.

Mrs. H: No, it took quite awhile. He got out twice for pretzels.

WHY WOMEN ARE BETTER THAN MEN . . .

Because men are like plungers; dey spend most of dere life in either a hardware store or da bathroom.

Because men are like bank accounts; vitout a lot of money, dey don't get any interest.

Because men are like lava lamps; dey're fun to look at, but not dat bright.

Because men are like laxatives; dey irritate da crap out of you!